Spiritual Messages
from the
Guardian
Spirit
of
Ryuho Okawa

The
DIVINE VOICE
of
SHAKYAMUNI BUDDHA

Videotaped July 12, 2013
Happy Science General Headquarters, Tokyo

RYUHO OKAWA
IRH Press

Contents

3

The Purpose of Founding the Happiness Realization Party

4

The "Religious Revolution" and
The "Political Revolution"

5

An Eternal Challenge Creating
A Utopia on Earth

6
The Truth about
Ryuho Okawa's Life Plan

7
The Relationship between Self-Power
And Outside Power, as Taught by

⚘ Closing Comments ⚘

8
His Disciples, Go on Turning
The Wheel of Dharma!

Preface

I have continuously published many spiritual messages. My main objective is to prove that the Spirit World exists, that the soul is your true self, and that God and Buddha exist, as well as the Bodhisattvas and angels who help them.

Devils are those who are governed by atheism and materialism, and who benefit by making others believe that their lives are limited to this world. Where they are, there will be a kind of political world favorable for people who live on the basis of the "selfish gene.*" But that is a boundless wasteland.

Among the spiritual messages that I have published are messages from the guardian spirits of those who are still alive on earth. However, some people are skeptical about this concept. Basically, thinking is a cerebral action for them. They are unable to understand how it is possible for their "guardian

---

* Richard Dawkins, a British ethologist and evolutionary biologist, formulated a hypothesis in his work, *The Selfish Gene* (1976), that reproduction and evolution of life is nothing more than the means by which 'selfish' genes survive. This hypothesis spread a materialistic view of life.

spirit" or subconscious mind to talk about their true thoughts.

I published the spiritual messages of the guardian spirits of the president and chief editor of a publishing company, and through an article, they have requested that I publish the spiritual messages from my own guardian spirit. Very well. Then I will not be able to say, "These messages are the opinions of the spirit and may contradict the views of the Happy Science Group."

The 87-minute conversation with my guardian spirit was made into this book, which is the answer to their request.

July 13, 2013
Master and CEO of the Happy Science Group
Ryuho Okawa

Interviewers from Happy Science:[*]

Eiichi Satomura
Senior Managing Director
Public Relations Division

Norihiro Uda
Vice Chairperson
Human Resources and Affiliated Projects

Yumiko Kanazawa
Director General of Education and Training Division

---

[*] Interviewers' professional titles represent their positions at the time of the interview. Their names are listed in the order that they appear in the transcript.

1

Responding to the Request from The Mass Media

The mass media began wanting to know what Ryuho Okawa really thinks

RYUHO OKAWA:

Today we have decided to record these spiritual messages for an unusual reason. In fact, a certain magazine recently published an article saying: "We would like to read spiritual messages from Ryuho Okawa's own guardian spirit." Of course, I think the writer was half in jest.

Happy Science has published many spiritual messages—not only from the spirits of people from the past, but also from the guardian spirits of people who are still alive and active in today's world. We call upon the guardian spirits of particular persons and publish their messages but we don't actually confirm whether the guardian spirit expresses the same opinions as the living person.

So far, the Japanese mass media have been using their power to refuse to report on religious matters, but recently they seem to have been unable to withhold their comments any longer. Ever since I published *Sugao No Okawa Ryuho* [The Real Side of Ryuho Okawa] (Tokyo: IRH Press, 2013), I get the feeling that the atmosphere has changed a little, and they seem to want to interview me.

Lately, we have been summoning the guardian spirits of famous people still alive today in order to find out their real thoughts and intentions, so obviously the media wonder what my own guardian spirit would say in such an interview. But since they are well aware that they are living right in the middle of daily muck without undertaking any spiritual training, they consider themselves unworthy of interviewing me directly, so instead they want us to publish this sort of interview.

Of course we don't intend to answer excessively mean requests. But as long as we publish books of spiritual messages from various guardian spirits, I am sure there will be wide public interest about who will appear if my own guardian spirit is summoned, and what kind of opinions he has to express.

My guardian spirit is one of "a number of faces On a statue of Buddha"

OKAWA:

In Buddhism, there are statues that have a number of faces on top of their heads, for instance the eleven-faced Goddess of Mercy and the thousand-armed Goddess of Mercy. I presume that in ancient times people knew, to some extent, that this was the expression of a spiritual truth.

Today we are going to conduct an interview with my own guardian spirit, and I think the spirit that is going to appear will be one of "a number of faces on a statue of Buddha." The reason there are a number of faces is that there are various kinds of people living in this world and in order to save each one of them, Buddha needs to have different aspects.

So who will appear if we summon the "guardian spirit of Ryuho Okawa"? When we summon the guardian spirits of people who are still active in the world, I think the most suitable spirit is selected and, from among their soul siblings*, probably the one who is most deeply involved with the person's current activities appears. So today, I want to do this in the same way, in an equally impartial manner.

---

* In principle, a human soul consists of six parts who take turns to be born into this world. One of them in the spirit world acts as the guardian spirit of the one who is currently born on earth.

What the media wants to know about me is probably this: "How much of the Happy Science and Happiness Realization Party's* activities are decided by Ryuho Okawa's own thoughts, as CEO of the group, as a human being? Are these consistent with the opinions of his guardian spirit? If not, how much of a gap is there between them? Or, is this something that cannot be identified since different spiritual influences are at work and various factors combine to create an idea?"

Actually I'm not sure if my thoughts coincide with those of my guardian spirit. If there is a huge discrepancy, I hope that our Public Relations Division will give some explanation [*laughs*]. If my guardian spirit's views are completely different from my own, they may have to explain that the disciples are at fault because they sometimes take charge and act recklessly, like the military authorities before World War II.† Please forgive me if it ends up like that.

We are undertaking many different activities, so we may not be able to cover everything. But anyway, I would like to call upon my own guardian spirit and see who will appear and what he has to say, in the same way as

---

* A political party established by Master Okawa. The party is backed by Happy Science.

† There are some who say that a part of the Imperial Japanese Army stationed in China went out of control, and brought about the Manchurian Incident and Sino-Japanese War (1937 - 45) that led to the Pacific War.

we do for other people, on an impartial footing. [*To the interviewers*] So please do your best.

Summoning Ryuho Okawa's guardian spirit

OKAWA:

Happy Science publishes different kinds of spiritual messages, including those from the guardian spirits of living people. As I am responsible for these publications, it is only natural that people outside are interested in knowing what my own guardian spirit has to say. So today, we are going to conduct a new experiment and receive spiritual messages from the guardian spirit of Ryuho Okawa.

[*Puts hands together in prayer and closes eyes.*]

The guardian spirit of Ryuho Okawa, Master of Happy Science and President of the Happiness Realization Party, please come down to Happy Science General Headquarters and tell us your true thoughts for the sake of others.

[*About 30 seconds of silence.*]

2

The Problems with the Japanese Constitution

Limitations of the current political system

EIICHI SATOMURA:
Good morning.

RYUHO OKAWA'S GUARDIAN SPIRIT:
Hmm.

SATOMURA:
Are you the guardian spirit of Master Ryuho Okawa?

OKAWA'S GUARDIAN SPIRIT:
Yes.

SATOMURA:
Thank you very much for granting us this precious opportunity to interview you for the first time in human history.

OKAWA'S GUARDIAN SPIRIT:
Hmm.

SATOMURA:

Then I'll start asking you some questions.

OKAWA'S GUARDIAN SPIRIT:

Hmm.

SATOMURA:

At the moment, the election of the House of Councilors is being held in Japan, and the streets are busy everywhere. Historically speaking, however, democracy and democratic elections have not always been the political norm.

In the lecture at the Celebration of the Lord's Descent [*"The Decision for Your Happiness," given on July 6, 2013*], Master Ryuho Okawa criticized the current political situation, where dishonesty is rampant. As his guardian spirit, how do you view the current Japanese politics and the election campaign?

OKAWA'S GUARDIAN SPIRIT:

People are making a big fuss about the elections. The Truth is obvious in my eyes, and there is no need to create such a stir.

SATOMURA:

Do you think there is something about the elections that goes against the will of Heaven?

OKAWA'S GUARDIAN SPIRIT:

I think that Japanese politics have been strongly influenced by modern European thinking, but that's not what politics are all about. You need to be aware that the current political system was not invented nor developed by Almighty beings, so it has its limits.

The basis for the "sovereignty of the people" is not Mentioned in the present Japanese Constitution

SATOMURA:

Here on earth and especially in Japan elections and the democratic system are considered supreme values. The mass media also make quite a point of this. What is your opinion of that?

OKAWA'S GUARDIAN SPIRIT:

I will point out two problems.

SATOMURA:

Yes.

OKAWA'S GUARDIAN SPIRIT:

Number one. The current Japanese Constitution guarantees the sovereignty of the people. That is fine. It was based on the United States Declaration of Independence, which states: "All men are created equal." The phrase "men are created" clearly implies that there is one who created them. This is an obvious fact.

In Christian societies, the equality of humans is expounded based on the premise that "Great God" or "the Creator" exists. Because humans are created equal by God, people discuss on the basis of equal rights and make rules according to their decisions. And they assume that what citizens have agreed on should be seen as conclusions representing the Will of God.

The Japanese Constitution followed suit but it does not describe the basis of the power of the "sovereignty of the people." If people have power solely because they are living in Japan, it means that they only have the right of abode and no other power. If the fact that people are living in a particular country is the sole basis of their power as citizens, then they will only have power based on their right of residence and there can be no grounds for universal values to arise. The current constitution has a defect in this respect.

If I would venture to say, the imperial system must represent God and constitute the basis of this power. However, under the current constitution, the emperor is merely a symbolic existence, one who renounced his divinity in a declaration*. He is a single human being equal to anybody else, only his position makes him the symbolic existence.

What is more, the emperor's areas of responsibility [*acts in matters of state*] are limited, and he is not allowed to do anything other than what is set down in the constitution. However, if there is a ruler whose retainers determine what should be done and what should not be done, he's just a puppet. In that case, we cannot say that the Constitution acknowledges the emperor as a representative of God, who created all men equal.

Therefore we can say that the current constitution has a flaw in it, that it does not outline the religious and philosophical basis for the "sovereignty of the people."

---

* An official statement issued by Emperor Showa on New Year's Day, 1946, the year after Japan's defeat. Until then, the emperor was defined as a sacred being according to the Meiji Constitution and worshiped like a god by Japanese people. In the statement, Emperor Showa denied his divinity declaring that it is an unrealistic notion for an emperor to be both a human being and a god.

The mass media are virtually acting As if they are God

OKAWA'S GUARDIAN SPIRIT:

There is another problem with the current constitution. Although it guarantees the freedom of religion, it contains certain articles that impose restrictions. On the other hand, there are no clauses that restrict the freedom of the press, though they are mentioned in the proposed drafts of a new constitution presented by some newspaper companies.

The constitution does not set down the responsibility of the media for failing to report something either. Therefore, in the current constitution, the rights with regard to the freedom of the press are deduced only from statements about the freedom of speech and publication.

However, the freedom of speech and publication are rights that are granted to all Japanese citizens. Obviously these are granted to religious organizations, as well as to other people. So we cannot find any particular reason that the mass media should have authority as a privileged class. Despite that, since they can use their power to influence the elections, it seems as though they are virtually acting as God.

It even seems that the criteria for good and bad come from the media. That being so, the mass media should indicate the basis for their judgments of good and bad, be it philosophy, morality or religion upon which their judgments are based. If they have no such grounds and judge things only on the basis of the question of whether or not they will sell or earn them publicity, then they are not qualified to criticize politicians as being populists.

I have so far pointed out two problems with regard to our constitution. If you want to know more, you can ask me further questions.

Democracy under the current constitution is In an atheistic atmosphere

SATOMURA:

From what you've just told us, we can see that Japan's democracy currently is not based on faith in God, although democracy is essentially a system that is allowed only on the basis of faith. We also understand that the media are taking God's place and position, and that today's democracy functions according to the media's intentions. From your point of view, does this situation exemplify impurity?

OKAWA'S GUARDIAN SPIRIT:

I'm not sure if I can really say that it's impure, but it's clear that it has flaws. Democracy under the current constitution seems to contain something that could be the basis for denying the existence of God, Buddha and the spiritual world, if we were to implement it as it is. I must say that is why it is creating the atmosphere of atheism in Japanese society, backed by scientific progressivism.

The constitution must state the fundamental Thoughts on the "state" and "human behavior"

NORIHIRO UDA:

The Happiness Realization Party was founded in 2009 and right after it was founded, Master Okawa released a new proposal for the Japanese Constitution (See *Shin Nihonkoku Kempo Shian* [A New Japanese Constitution A Proposal] (Tokyo: IRH Press, 2009). It talks about faith in the preamble, and the freedom of religion in Article 2.

This draft proposal was written in one day. Usually, writing a draft proposal for a constitution takes at least six months or a year, but since this was written in a day, we were surprised and so was everybody else in society.

From what I've heard from you so far, I presume that you made some suggestions or gave guidance in the creation of this proposal. Were you involved in it? If so, how much were you involved in creating it?

OKAWA'S GUARDIAN SPIRIT:

I'm not interested in worldly tasks like that. I have certain ideas, and these were manifested in the proposal in certain forms of expression.

I think the current constitution is like a collection of different ideas accumulated over the last 200 years of the modern era, and the text and philosophy are far from sublime "eternal ideals." There is no philosophy as its basis, but there is an objective. Obviously it is imbued with the objective of "what kind of state Japan should be."

Actually, this constitution is trying to make Japan into a "state with no God" and to take away the dignity of the Japanese soul. I have the impression that it clearly has this sort of objective inherent in it.

However, it is traditionally believed that Japan is a country where God and Buddha reside, and the Japanese people have always believed that they were the children of God or Buddha. The constitutional and legal scholars may think of the constitution as based solely on modern technical legal theory, but I believe that a constitution is not necessary unless it indicates the fundamental ideas which serve as the basis for the state and human behavior.

Problems that could arise from articles of law Referred to in the current constitution

OKAWA'S GUARDIAN SPIRIT:
The current constitution also contains many parts that are considered as articles of law.

• *About the Imperial Family*

Take the imperial system, for example. Although this could be controversial, there would be consistency if the constitution stated: "Japan is a nation where people believe in the emperor as the proper successor to *Amaterasu-O-Mikami* [*the Sun Goddess*], following their faith in the Sun Goddess." But this is not actually the case. It just describes what the emperor can do and how the succession to the Imperial Throne takes place, which should essentially be dealt with in the Imperial Household Law.

• *About the one-year budget*

There are many such examples with regard to other rights. This is because so many unnecessary provisions were added to the constitution and it is one reason that this country has problems running itself.

For example, the one-year budget is determined by the constitution and this is why there is a budget deficit. If this were not set down in the constitution, the state would naturally strive to make a profit just like any other business. If the country were run by politicians with management skills, there wouldn't be a budget deficit.

However, the constitution says that all tax revenue that comes in each year must be used by the end of that year. This being so, all the government officials must follow this rule. In that instance, when the economy is booming, national finances may not be in the red, but the economy goes through certain cycles and fluctuates between strong and weak, and in a weak economy there is a shortfall of revenue from taxes. This is a natural consequence.

What is more, if all the tax revenue from the strong years is used up completely each year, nothing will be stored as savings and, as a result, a budget deficit will only accumulate. I have to say that this is an obvious flaw in the constitution.

I have cited just a few examples, but I suppose there are many other problems with the constitution.

For 70 years, Japan has remained suppressed in the Same position as it was under American occupation

SATOMURA:

You have astutely pointed out some problems with the Japanese Constitution. Actually it is said that the current Japanese Constitution was imposed by GHQ* after World War II. When it was introduced, were there any suggestions from the heavenly world, or was there any inspiration that came from God?

OKAWA'S GUARDIAN SPIRIT:

The Japanese spirit world was definitely not involved. Now you may wonder if there was any guidance from a global perspective, and of course there was, from those

---

* The General Headquarters (GHQ) rejected the Outline of Constitution Revision created by the Japanese government because they thought that the draft was insufficient to democratize Japan. GHQ prepared and forced their own draft (the so-called "MacArthur draft") onto the Japanese government. This draft developed into the Constitution of Japan.

who thought of benefitting the U.S., since the central power of the allied forces was the United States. The constitution also includes ideas that take China and the Korean Peninsula into consideration. But from the perspective of God or Buddha, there is no doubt that this constitution was enacted basically to retaliate against Japan.

SATOMURA:

Watching from the heavenly world, at the point when this constitution was imposed, did you already conceive that it would have to be changed one day?

OKAWA'S GUARDIAN SPIRIT:

Of course I did. In a way, the Japanese nation was already "destroyed" when it was forced to surrender unconditionally and its emperor declared he was a mere human. So we must found a new nation.

After the war, for 70 years Japan has remained in the same position as when it was suppressed under American occupation. So it is only natural that Japanese people should decide on the ideal state of their own country.

As for the details, I think it's fine to continue adding other ideas and making improvements in the future, but for the general principles I think you need to present the proper ideals.

Shin Nihonkoku Kempo Shian [*as already cited*] does not come from my own ideas directly, but I agree with the overall ideas of the general principles.

The spiritual background of the proposal for A new Japanese Constitution

SATOMURA:

We have heard that Master Ryuho Okawa's proposal for a new constitution was inspired by Prince Shotoku*. Is it all right to assume that the proposal was created with Prince Shotoku as the central guide?

OKAWA'S GUARDIAN SPIRIT:

I think he was the main guiding spirit giving direct instructions for the writing of the actual proposal, but he must have communicated with other spirits about the basic ideas.

---

* Prince Shotoku (574 - 622)
A son of Japan's 31st emperor, Yomei. He assumed the regency of the 33rd emperor, Empress Suiko, at the age of 19. He was well-versed in academic studies and contributed to promoting Buddhism as a devout Buddhist. The Seventeen-article constitution, which he established in 604 based on Buddhism and Confucianism, aimed to create a nation ruled by virtue. This constitution had a big impact on later generations, serving Japan as its spiritual backbone.

SATOMURA:

Would you please tell me who the "other spirits" are?

OKAWA'S GUARDIAN SPIRIT:

They are the central guiding spirits of Happy Science.

SATOMURA:

Actually, Happy Science receives guidance and support from many high spirits...

OKAWA'S GUARDIAN SPIRIT:

It is said that in total there are about 500 spirits giving Happy Science guidance, but only around 10-20 of them are constantly involved in the main issues. They are the "executives" of the guiding spirit group.

SATOMURA:

Is Jesus Christ involved, for example?

OKAWA'S GUARDIAN SPIRIT:

Jesus is not involved much. Although Japan was defeated by Christian countries, Jesus was not really involved in formulating the Japanese Constitution after the war. And he didn't play a particularly big role in creating the new proposal, either. But he does approve of the basic ideas, of course.

SATOMURA:

Can the same thing be said of the Japanese Shinto gods, including *Ame-no-Minakanushi-no-Kami* [literally, the God Ruling the Center of Heaven]?

OKAWA'S GUARDIAN SPIRIT:

Yes, of course.

Arguing about contradictions in The "peace constitution"

YUMIKO KANAZAWA:

I would like to know more about the problems with the current constitution. Women tend to feel more fear and therefore get emotional when they are told, "It is safer to keep the current Japanese Constitution since it's a peace constitution. A war could easily break out if Article 9 is amended."

However, I believe that if we truly seek peace, we must think about "peace based on justice." It shouldn't be something that is realized after having compromised with evil forces or having given in to them. So please explain to us the problems with the "peace constitution" from the perspective of true justice, centered on the will of God or Buddha.

• *Is the U.S. entitled to enforce A "peace constitution"?*

OKAWA'S GUARDIAN SPIRIT:

Let's look at it from a different angle. The American Constitution guarantees each individual the right of possession of a gun, and all American citizens are granted the right to protect themselves and their families with a gun. As a result, there have been many cases of murder by shooting in the United States. But since this right has been placed under protection for over 200 years from the time of the founding of the U.S., it cannot be changed so easily and is now causing Americans a lot of trouble.

Given that the Japanese Constitution was written by Americans, if its pacifist views were right, then the U.S. would not have been able to retain the Seventh Fleet. And if Americans love peace that much, then they should ban guns from their homes as is the case in Japan; that would certainly bring about a more peaceful society.

Of course, it is possible to preach pacifism as the Japanese Constitution suggests, and it would be totally understandable if those who practice pacifism insisted on that kind of peace constitution. However, it is somewhat questionable when those who cannot even act on for peace insist on how to achieve it.

The peace they are talking about is not peace for Japan. It is simply peace for themselves, for those who are imposing pacifism on Japan. For thieves or robbers, for example, a society where each family does not have guns is considered peaceful, isn't it?

SATOMURA:
Yes, that's true.

• *Are countries with nuclear weapons entitled to Impose pacifism on other countries?*

OKAWA'S GUARDIAN SPIRIT:
And for banks, a society where guns are not in circulation is considered peaceful. Therefore, if people enforce pacifism on others out of a selfish desire to protect their own interests, we have to assume that their motives are not necessarily good.

Moreover, the United Nations has been directing the post war world regime and all the permanent members of the Security Council arm themselves with nuclear weapons. They need to discuss seriously whether or not this goes against pacifism. If they insist that this doesn't go against pacifism, then we cannot say that the appeals for non-proliferation are contributing to promoting world peace.

If they themselves disarm and declare that the permanent members will abandon all nuclear weapons, then it is fair and right to say that other countries should not possess nuclear weapons either and that there must be no further proliferation. However, they are saying: "While we have the right to keep our nuclear weapons, other countries are still too immature and are therefore not allowed to have them." And to maintain their dominant position, they are telling other countries they should not possess nuclear weapons.

So the peace they are talking about is no more than a peace that only serves to protect the interests of the former allies. From philosophical, religious, and ethical standpoints, what they are saying is simply unreasonable.

The root of a masochistic view of history — *The idea that only Japan must renounce Any war capability*

OKAWA'S GUARDIAN SPIRIT:
I think both approaches are possible, but if not possessing capability of war as set forth in Article 9 of the Japanese Constitution ensures peace in Japan, then the same idea should also apply to our neighboring country, China.

China already possesses various nuclear weapons and other weapons of aggression, and is still continuing to develop them. But renouncing such weapons would certainly ensure peace for them. As long as they possess these weapons, there is a higher possibility of China being attacked by other countries. Therefore, not having them would be more conducive to peace.

The same is true for North Korea. If such a small country develops nuclear missiles, obviously there will be more possibility of larger countries imposing sanctions on it, so for North Korea, it would be more conducive to peace not to have nuclear missiles. In this case, it is quite reasonable to say that getting rid of their nuclear weapons will bring peace.

However, if you disregard their behavior and just think that Japan's renouncing its war capability is the path to secure world peace, then I must say that is the very source of a masochistic view of history for Japan.

SATOMURA:

You have astutely pointed out problems with the Japanese Constitution that change our perspective on our so-called "peace constitution." Thank you very much. From what you have just said, I could sense your very strong determination, not to amend the current Constitution, but to establish a new one.

3

The Purpose of Founding
The Happiness Realization Party

The first major mission was to educate the people

SATOMURA:

Now we would also like to talk about the Happiness Realization Party that Master Ryuho Okawa founded in 2009. Around the same time as Master Okawa wrote the proposal for a new Japanese Constitution, he founded the Happiness Realization Party. At that time, Master Okawa said that the political party had been founded a little earlier than was planned.

Was the founding of the Happiness Realization Party in 2009 and the start of its activities a calling, the will of Heaven, or your will? Or was it Master Okawa's own idea based on his experiences in this lifetime?

OKAWA'S GUARDIAN SPIRIT:

Considering various factors, including the activities of Happy Science and its capabilities, it was obvious that it would be extremely difficult to amass the power to be able to assume the reins of government at that time in 2009. But there was a major mission to educate the people first.

One of the reasons for this was that at that time the Liberal Democratic Party, which ruled Japan after World War II, began to seem as if they did not have much time left.

Another reason was that North Korea was developing and testing nuclear missiles. The Japanese government seems as though it has been trying hard for years to solve the issue of abduction of Japanese citizens by their neighboring country, North Korea. The number of abductees is uncertain, whether it be one hundred or several hundred, but Japan has been conducting campaigns to bring back its citizens. In these circumstances, North Korea was moving forward with its nuclear program.

This was something that would carry on year after year, so it needed to be stopped at the earliest possible time, otherwise the situation would only have gotten worse. While the issue was supposed to be discussed at the Six-Party Talks, the country which was negotiating directly with North Korea was China, which is virtually colonizing it. So we thought that it was impossible for the wolf to keep an eye on the sheep.

Therefore, seeing the Liberal Democratic Party crumbling in 2009, the decision was made to imbue

Japan with a new philosophy and strengthen public opinion in Japan.

The opinions and activities of the Happiness Realization Party have changed The course of Japan

OKAWA'S GUARDIAN SPIRIT:

It is, of course, very clear that entering the political arena is an extremely difficult task since Happy Science is now also pouring its energy into educational projects, as well as overseas missionary work by opening local branches abroad. However, everything has a beginning. Without taking the first step, you cannot achieve growth or success.

At the very least, it is an undeniable fact that the opinions and activities of the Happiness Realization Party have influenced this country to a certain extent, and have changed the course it is taking. No one can deny this.

If the Happiness Realization Party had not existed since 2009, it is highly possible that most of the mass media would have tried to find a way for Japan to survive, going in the direction of building a friendly relationship with China. But that would have forced Japan to decide whether it was going to be taken under China's protection, though Japan may have achieved great economic success through it.

If China were trying to expand its power on the basis of righteous thoughts and in the direction of bringing happiness to all humanity, I wouldn't disagree with that option and it would be fine for Japan to follow China. However, if we look at China's history over the last few decades, including what they are doing now, it's obvious that China is moving far from the will of God or Buddha.

It's just intolerable to remain quiet while Japan submits to a nation that is going against the will of God or Buddha, and is assimilated into that power. That's what brings out the power of our strong determination to intervene.

If China was the role model for the world, the [*pro-China*] foreign policy that the Democratic Party of Japan administration pursued* would have been an option. But China's current attitude is not that of a model country for the world. That's why we have put forward a stern "No!" against Japan moving towards that direction.

In this regard, Happy Science may have shouldered a very heavy burden. But things start from an idea. By expressing an idea, I believe that we can pose a question to other people about whether their ideas are just.

God or Buddha is trying to stand in China's way

•*If a materialistic nation had ruled the world*

OKAWA'S GUARDIAN SPIRIT:

It is true that the U.S. has many problems, but imagine what would have happened if, just around 20 years ago, the Soviet Union had won the conflict against the U.S. and their values had ruled the entire world. I presume that the tendency to suppress people's freedom, deprive them of human rights, and for political leaders to oppress the people arbitrarily would have spread throughout the world.

At that time, the U.S. was suffering from "twin deficits" — both a budget deficit and an international trade deficit. But still it kept expanding its military to compete with the Soviet Union until finally, the Soviet

---

* DPJ is a Japanese liberal party which was in power from September 2009 to December 2012. Prime Minister Yukio Hatoyama of DPJ placed more importance on China than on the U.S. and jeopardized the Japan-U.S. ties.

Union's economy collapsed without waging war. As a result, the U.S. was able to bring an end to the Cold War without any loss of life. With regard to this matter, the Will of God and Buddha was clearly on the side of the United States.

•*China is now trying to do what the former Soviet Union did*

Right now, China is trying to do the same thing that the Soviet Union once tried, and God or Buddha is trying to stand in its way.

At the moment your power on earth may still be limited, but you shouldn't think that you may stay small. However small an acorn may be, once it falls to the ground and grows, it will eventually turn into a giant tree, tens of meters high. The same is true of you. Even if you are a small acorn now, I assure you that you can grow into a tall tree. Until then, you will need to devote much sweat and tears, and make a lot of effort.

We cannot allow Japan to fall Under the rule of the devil

UDA:

We thought that the purposes for founding the Happiness Realization Party were to turn Japan into a religious nation and restore true freedom of religion, as well as to emphasize the importance of national defense and amend Article 9 of the Japanese Constitution*.

But listening to you now, I understood that this political party was founded to put up the holy flag and declare, not only in Japan but also to the world, "Here lies justice. Here lies conscience. And here lies the source of all kinds of righteousness." I really felt again that this party was created out of such huge aspirations.

However, at present, Japan and other developed countries in the world are basically democratic countries based on the voting system. You have just mentioned the example of the acorn, but under such a system, how can we tell the truth to many people? Many high spirits point out our weak faith as disciples and our weak missionary work. But being still a small group,

---

* An article in the Constitution of Japan that declares pacifism. It consists of three elements: renunciation of war, non-maintenance of the armed forces and denial of the right of belligerency.

how can we gain recognition from many people? We would greatly appreciate it if you could give us some advice on this matter.

OKAWA'S GUARDIAN SPIRIT:

Let me tell you something first. While there are countries closer to American values and countries closer to Chinese values, this is not a fight between freedom and equality. I want you to know this.

I would also like to state clearly that, in Chinese values, there is something different from the equality that God or Buddha approves of, and that there are forces at work, trying to turn Heaven into Hell. Their values are clearly different from the idea that each soul exercises freedom and grows as a child of God or Buddha.

If all humans are the children of God or Buddha, it is only natural that they should have an equal right to seek unrestrained development. However, communism has ruled China for too long. I must say that the equality according to the Chinese values is one that is intentionally created, so that a handful of politicians can keep the people silent.

Although China is in transition economically, its basic attitude or fundamental principles haven't yet changed. It still maintains a regime in which just a small number of leaders are oppressing and exploiting the overwhelming majority, and finds it natural to invade other countries and incorporate them into its country out of selfish desires. This situation is far from the freedom or happiness that God or Buddha approves of. Instead, it is the result of self-development of those who believe that this earthly world is the only place to live.

So, although the situation may look like a conflict between freedom and equality, in reality, it is a battle between the powers that believe in God or Buddha, and the powers that believe in the devil. The second Cold War is now occurring.

I definitely cannot allow Japan, this country which God and Buddha protect, to fall under the devil's rule. This is why the Happiness Realization Party was founded.

4

The "Religious Revolution" and The "Political Revolution"

The mass media's "gossip democracy" Promotes the rule of the devil

SATOMURA:

Right now, some of the Japanese bad-mouthed mass media are saying that none of the candidates of the Happiness Realization Party will get seats in the House of Councilors election [*in the following week*]. Do you think that we should continue engaging in this fight without giving in to such voices?

OKAWA'S GUARDIAN SPIRIT:

If the mass media are capable of embracing the Will of God or Buddha, the results will turn in that direction, but if they are in tune with the voice of the devil, the results will be drawn in a direction that will please the devil. So what they say will come back to them. This election will pose questions about the raison d'être of the mass media themselves, and whether they have the insight to judge good from bad.

Do they want to drive this country forward in the direction of creating a nation where people recognize the existence of God or Buddha, or a nation where the devil rules?

The fundamental principle of the mass media is, to portray it in a good light, doubt and criticism or, to portray it in a bad light, speaking ill of others. If they like "gossip democracy" best, then they will find it comfortable to live in a country ruled by the devil. If they really find value in this form of democratic system in itself, I must say that they are living in fundamental ignorance.

If, in the end, democracy has the power to make people shine in the best possible way, it is possible to evaluate it positively. However, if democracy is a system that ends up making people corrupt and pushing them into the devil's camp, moral guidance is needed. Those who can give this moral guidance are the religions and the people who have a religious disposition.

The final goal is to realize a Buddhaland Utopia

KANAZAWA:

So the noble cause for the Happiness Realization Party and for this House of Councilors election is to manifest the Will of God or Buddha on earth, and not the will of the devil. Is that what you mean?

OKAWA'S GUARDIAN SPIRIT:

The final goal is to realize what you call a "Buddhaland Utopia." Of course, this is not an easy task. However, as long as the constitution, the political system, or political ideals are connected to the eternal ideals of humankind, though the realization of a Buddhaland Utopia may still be a far-off dream, it is important that you keep on making efforts to get closer to it, generation after generation.

The reason a spiritual revolution is necessary in The era of the second Cold War

UDA:

As I listen to you, I feel yet again that politics and religion are not separate. Since the beginning of the year, Master Okawa has started using the term "spiritual revolution." But if we look at his past lectures, we can see that for over 20 years he has been saying that, first of all, we have to establish an age of spirituality. He has been saying this ever since he founded Happy Science.

This year, Master Okawa is again giving teachings on spiritual revolution. From your point of view, what are the essence of spiritual revolution and the religious significance of promoting the revolution? Please instruct us on these points.

OKAWA'S GUARDIAN SPIRIT:

As I said, right now the second Cold War has started between the camp centered on the U.S. and the camp centered on China, and we must win this conflict. And there is one more point that I must add.

In the U.S. camp, there are underlying concepts of freedom and equality, and the philosophy that humans are God's creation, but there is also a negative side to this. Though American philosophy was introduced from Europe, the U.S. itself is still a young country with a short history. Immigrants started settling there only 400 years ago, and it has only been about 200 years since the U.S. was founded as a country. A country with such a short history has now become the world superpower.

Therefore, I must say that what comes out from America does not cover the entire intellectual heritage of humanity in a cultural and historical sense. To put it in more concrete terms, because of its short history the U.S. has not yet produced anybody worthy of being called "the progenitor of the human race," "the founder of a worldwide religion," "the father of philosophy" or "the father of a global ideology." Such a country is now trying to implement the traditions it inherited from Europe in a pragmatic way. This is the current world situation. However, there is something lacking.

Japan, on the other hand, has a recorded history of at least 3,000 years. During that time, different gods have descended and the country has already absorbed many world religions through its history.

The American values alone are not enough. It is important that a country like Japan, which harbors a fundamental philosophy of God or Buddha, prospers as a nation of freedom. We use the words "spiritual revolution," because unless democracy is imbued with spirituality, it will end up merely as pragmatic worldly activities of humans. Then it will be far from an eternal ideal.

The difficulty of running two Revolutions simultaneously

SATOMURA:

I now really feel that the political activities of the Happiness Realization Party have an enormously lofty goal. But unfortunately, in this world, we still haven't achieved the good results that we had hoped for. Being ordinary people, at times we followers and the party members feel discouraged. Please give us some words of encouragement.

OKAWA'S GUARDIAN SPIRIT:

You are now taking on the challenge of two revolutions. The first is a religious revolution, or to put it in another way, a spiritual revolution.

A lot of Japanese people, after losing in World War II, have lost faith and are seeking materialistic prosperity. So we need to help them regain faith and make them realize that, unless they believe in the spiritual world and the existence of God or Buddha, they cannot lead a truly valuable life as a human being. This is the religious revolution, or the spiritual revolution, which is the first stage.

But although this stage has not yet been accomplished, you are simultaneously trying to launch a "political revolution," which is the second stage. So currently, the two kinds of revolution are taking place at the same time. This is what makes the current political activities so difficult.

If the first revolution had been completed, the second one would be a little easier. But you haven't achieved total victory in the first revolution. Although Happy Science has gained a certain amount of power in Japan, it is still regarded merely as one of the influential religious groups among many others.

Many other religious groups believe in teachings that in effect are no different from materialism. They are not even sure whether God or Buddha really exists, or whether the other world exists. Some Buddhist sects even teach that when you die, everything is finished.

The job of politicians is to manifest Religious ideals in a tangible way

OKAWA'S GUARDIAN SPIRIT:
In this situation, such religions base their thinking on the constitution. The situation has turned around from

what it should be. Their task has become, "to protect the so-called 'fundamental human rights' which are included in the constitution after World War II," rather than "to protect what religion should be teaching." In short, those religions have been persuaded into following politics, and are now being used to support political activities. This is how it seems.

The concept of fundamental human rights can include the idea of protecting the rights of the majority and protecting the rights of the individual. Although both ideas are important, it can be said that, if you neglect the common good and focus too much on the individual, you will eventually tend to harbor a leftist ideology. However, the basic idea we should adopt is that while promoting the happiness of the majority, it is also important to pay attention to the rights of minorities and protect them. This is a difficult task, but you must carry out these activities simultaneously.

In the process of manifesting justice, of course situations will always arise where you must choose between the two, between justice for one party and justice for another. In such a dilemma, how would you create a better outcome? To achieve this and gain concrete results is the essential work of politicians. Basically, politicians must accept the ideals of a religious leader and work to manifest them in a tangible way.

By making full use of worldly wisdom, it is important to think about how to ensure the happiness of the majority and maintain development while, at the same time, protecting those who have fallen through the cracks in this development. Politicians must rack their brains as to how to proceed further with this difficult task in a tangible way.

Heaven's will is expressed in This year's summer heat

OKAWA'S GUARDIAN SPIRIT:
This year, for example, the rainy season was over sooner than usual, and in many places in Japan temperatures were over 35°C. Heat waves continue and there were even cities that reached as high as 39°C. Every day, many people are taken to hospitals suffering from heat stroke and dehydration, and die. Such occurrences are dealt with as merely a natural phenomenon, but to prevent such deaths, it is very important to create a system that provides cheap electricity.

In fact, you need to know that Heaven's will is being expressed here, in this short rainy season and the arrival of a hot summer. This is a message telling you: "Know that a stable electricity supply will create a better society to live in, and will protect the lives of elderly people and children."

The same is true of the earthquake disaster. Although it was also an expression of Heaven's will, people are interpreting it in a wrong, materialistic way. They simply clamor to abolish all nuclear power plants, so that no accidents will ever occur again and their worldly lives will be preserved. However, Heaven's will does not point in that direction. We are telling people that the future is not to be found in that way. They need to be aware of this.

The mission of disciples is to spread the messages From Heaven and increase the number of believers

SATOMURA:

So we must keep on working after knowing Heaven's will? Is that what you mean?

OKAWA'S GUARDIAN SPIRIT:

What you are working on may appear contrary to the "justice as a common illusion" that the media created, but the truth is that you are listening to a voice that the media cannot hear.

Those who listen to the voice of Heaven are always in small numbers. However, it is possible to spread those messages and increase the number of people who believe in it. This is the task of disciples.

KANAZAWA & SATOMURA:

Right.

5

An Eternal Challenge Creating A Utopia on Earth

Turning the whole of Japan into a country of God and Buddha

UDA:

To achieve that we need to convey the will of Heaven continuously, no matter what, even if we are still a minority. I think endurance is important in this endeavor. What are your thoughts on this?

OKAWA'S GUARDIAN SPIRIT:

Of course, the ultimate goal is to spread our teachings, not only in Japan but to every corner of the world, so this is not solely a question of one country. But before going to that level, we must first change basic attitudes in Japan. So what we are doing right now is not all about winning or losing an election. Our work will not come to an end once we have established a tiny political party. We are doing this to turn the whole of Japan into a country of God and Buddha.

And changing this country alone is not enough. This course of action is clearly indicated. This movement aims to create a Buddhaland Utopia based on the new teachings of God and Buddha, in other Asian countries as well as in African and Western countries, and elsewhere. Viewed from this perspective, this is not the kind of movement that will end after just one generation. You must know this.

This is an eternal challenge. We do not think of our victory simply as obtaining one or two, or five seats in the Diet, or creating a tiny political party. We must continue doing this until we have turned the entire country into a nation of faith.

You must stand up against evil countries That oppress their people

KANAZAWA:
I think everyone listening to you now will be able to feel a great sense of mission.

Now, during this heat wave of nearly 40°C, many followers who have been aiming to become Angels of Light [*Bodhisattvas*] through religious activities are earnestly making an effort every day to realize the Lord's ideals in the political arena. So I would like to know if there is also a path to becoming an Angel of Light through political activities.

Also, from the standpoint of the future, say 500 or 1,000 years from now, what kind of spiritual meaning will our current activities and the four-year activities of the Happiness Realization Party have? Will you please give us teachings about this?

OKAWA'S GUARDIAN SPIRIT:

Major problems that Japan is now facing are, aside from the issue of nuclear power plants, controversial issues that have arisen in the process of discussing the potential amendments to the constitution, especially to Article 9. These are the issues regarding "how to convince people to approve the establishment of defense forces and national security forces" and "how to convince people to approve of the threat these forces may pose to our neighboring countries, in the context of their historical recognition."

Of course, I neither approve of nor favor a world where people kill each other. I think that a world where such happenings do not occur is desirable. However, if a country rises up which expands an evil regime based on evil thoughts, and if tens of millions of people or more are oppressed, persecuted, sent to concentration camps and killed, then even the children of God must rise up against this.

We cannot help evil grow. Although I do not condone a world in which people kill each other, you must realize that allowing evil forces to spread under the rule of the devil and not being able to stop them is another form of evil. In this sense, the righteous ones must be strong, and your voices must be stronger than the mass media, which are being manipulated by the devil! I dare say this to you.

If debates and popular movements are not enough, There can also be "God's army"

OKAWA'S GUARDIAN SPIRIT:
It is good to create a world where there is no killing. But sometimes it is wrong to assume that such a world will manifest automatically if you stand by and do nothing.

If there is actually somebody who is trying to develop evil aims, and if you can deter him with your words, do it! If you can change an evil regime by launching a popular movement, that is fine, too! But if these are not enough to stop the evil, there can also be "God's army"! I dare say that to you.

SATOMURA:

So is it correct to assume that this is a time when the Happiness Realization Party needs to show the significance of God's army?

OKAWA'S GUARDIAN SPIRIT:

Exactly. If you don't do it now, then who will? How much influence do Buddhism and Christianity have in Japan today? And, how strong are the convictions and determination of the existing political parties?

By amending Article 96, Prime Minister Abe is Virtually aiming to abolish the constitution

OKAWA'S GUARDIAN SPIRIT:

The current head of the Liberal Democratic Party, Prime Minister Abe, is aiming to amend the Japanese Constitution. To achieve that, he is first trying to change Article 96, so that an amendment to the constitution can be proposed with a majority of over 50 percent of all the members of each House and a two-thirds majority is no longer needed. This would mean that proposing a motion to change the constitution would be as simple as changing other ordinary laws.

However, most people work during the day and very few people watch live broadcasts of the Diet sessions. As a result, numerous bills are passed without people noticing. People may discover the decisions made in the Diet later in newspapers or some other news source, but they do not get a chance to express their opinions. Therefore, once they elect certain politicians and approve those politicians as the representatives of the people, they have to leave everything to the arbitrary decisions the politicians make.

The current prime minister is trying to put the constitution on a similar level. He is trying to set up a situation where he can change the articles of the constitution one after another by a majority vote [*over 50 percent*], just like any other law. This would no longer be the amendment of the constitution but virtually equivalent to the abolition of the constitution itself. This is what he seems to be aiming for. In a Diet session, tens or even hundreds of laws are passed, and if the constitution can be changed at this rate, it would be possible to have the same effect as abolishing it.

However, it is not so easy for citizens to take back the authority once they have entrusted it to the politicians, or to turn them around. If people wanted to oppose a specific constitutional amendment, they would have to vote for another party in the next election so that the new government would add yet another amendment and change things. If such kind of process continues forever, then there would be no way we can expect a stable order in the nation.

What Prime Minister Abe is lacking in now is a philosophy, a religion, the mirror in his mind that reflects the essential Will of God or Buddha. He cannot abolish and recreate the constitution merely on the basis of the ideal, "Towards a Beautiful Country"! He must know that unless he has a grander and more convincing fundamental philosophy as the backbone, he cannot take on the responsibility of changing the constitution! I dare to say this.

SATOMURA:
Thank you very much.

6

The Truth about Ryuho Okawa's Life Plan

Communism — a religion created by the devil

SATOMURA:

I would now like to ask you about Master Ryuho Okawa, who founded the Happiness Realization Party and is also the CEO of the entire Happy Science Group. Master Ryuho Okawa is now active in two arenas, as a religious leader and a political revolutionary, but what exactly does this signify? Is it possible for these two activities to be compatible in today's society? I would like to hear your thoughts on this point.

OKAWA'S GUARDIAN SPIRIT:

As in religions, in the communist revolution too, there were ideological battles to infiltrate the minds of citizens of a country, and often the people of other countries, with a certain ideology. In a way, it may have been a religious movement in a different form; indeed, communism is a religion created by the devil. The religion created by the devil has manifested in the political arena as communism.

In fact, evil forces are engaged in a religious movement and a political movement simultaneously. The devil's side is also involved in two movements, a movement to spread the devil's thoughts and a movement to implement a system akin to communism.

Therefore, God and Buddha's side must also carry out both religious and political activities, otherwise we cannot win this battle against evil forces. These are my thoughts.

Three reasons why Ryuho Okawa Was born in Japan

SATOMURA:
With this mission, Master Ryuho Okawa was born in Japan in this lifetime. So why did he choose Japan?

•*Revising the history of colonial rule by whites*

OKAWA'S GUARDIAN SPIRIT:
The reason for this is related to the plan for world history. The imperialist colonial rule of white supremacy has continued for nearly 500 years. Currently, the details are not really known to the world, but if these are written

clearly in the history books or school textbooks, people will see that it was really a cruel and tragic history.

Europeans turned African countries into their colonies and exploited the black people as their slaves. Although these people are the same human beings, they were sold like cattle to the United States. It is wrong to think that God or Buddha would keep silent about this. So, one of his missions is to revise the history of colonial rule by white races.

• *The fight against communism and the Reformation of the Islamic world*

Another mission is to fight against communism. Centered around China and Russia, the operations to contain God and Buddha have been undertaken by materialistic thinking under the name of the communist movement, so he has to fight against these operations.

There is also a mission to reform the Islamic world. About 1,400 years ago, Muhammad was sent to earth to create a new religion to spread the messages of Allah, but there are many points to improve in their philosophy, which connects religion, politics and the economy.

There is a pressing need to completely revise the form of their religion.

Viewed from these three points, if one thinks of the best place to send out his messages from, he would end up choosing Japan.

SATOMURA:

Thank you very much for revealing this truth.

Starting his life as a religious leader Was not an option

SATOMURA:

Please forgive me for asking you quite a bold question again. In this lifetime, Master Ryuho Okawa was born in Kawashima-cho [*now Yoshinogawa city*], a small town in the mountains in Tokushima Prefecture, far from Tokyo, the political and economic heart of Japan. Then as a young man, he made every effort to enter the University of Tokyo* and, after graduation, worked for a trading company. This does not appear to be a straightforward

---

* The most prestigious, nationally-funded academic institution in Japan. It was also the first modern university established in Japan.

path to becoming a religious leader, but rather a life that took a roundabout route. Please tell us why he took this life path?

OKAWA'S GUARDIAN SPIRIT:

Let me answer your last question first. If he had spent time undergoing spiritual training in an existing traditional religion or a new religion, he would have continued using the ways of thinking and spiritual training he had learned there. He wanted to avoid that risk. This seems to be one reason.

Usually, it is hard for people to abandon what they have learned. So if he had been born into a temple of a particular Buddhist sect and, after having undergone some spiritual training there, had founded his own religion, he would probably not have been able to go beyond that religion. It would have been impossible for him to launch a grand-scale global religious movement with the level of influence he currently has in mind. In this sense, the option of starting to live as a religious leader straightaway was excluded from the very beginning.

Acquiring the "self-help" spirit

OKAWA'S GUARDIAN SPIRIT:

Another question you asked is why he chose to be born in the countryside, not in a city, then forged himself by making worldly efforts just like an ordinary person, spending time working in another occupation before he became a religious leader. The reason for this is, as you may already have learned through numerous teachings, we wanted him to master the law of cause and effect or, to put it another way, to acquire the spirit of self-help.

If he had been born into a wealthy family like, for example, that of Mr. Yukio Hatoyama*, the first prime minister of the former Democratic Party of Japan administration, he would not have been able to impress people by teaching the spirit of self-help because it would simply have been a parlor teaching. In reality that would have been impossible. In that case, the teaching would only have been an opinion by someone who has been given everything. That's why we wanted him to experience this spirit for himself.

---

* The Hatoyamas is a family that has been continuing from the 17th century. Yukio Hatoyama's mother comes from the Ishibashis, the family that founded Bridgestone, the world's largest tire manufacturer. According to a media report, Mr. Hatoyama was given political donations of 15 million yen a month from his mother, for seven or eight years.

This is also an attitude that God or Buddha expects of humans. The world population is now increasing from seven billion to 10 billion and, although we want to save many people, if this increasing population relied solely on governments, the UN or the international community, it would be too difficult to save them all. So we need to teach them always to remember the basic responsibilities of being human: to work on their own, travel on their own two feet, catch fish with their own net and produce food by tilling the land with their own hoe.

Basically, any organization can work if it is formed of people who have the spirit of "self-help." It is important that, in a self-help society, competent people are selected fairly to be the leaders. And if there are any who fall through the cracks of society, it is important to deal with them with mercy.

Forcing "unwelcome good intentions" will corrupt Those who can help themselves

OKAWA'S GUARDIAN SPIRIT:

At present, however, out of the desire to acquire more votes, the mass media and various political parties are trying to use the same approach that they take for people who are unable to help themselves, on those who actually can help themselves. At a glance, this may seem like a good intention, but forcing unwelcome good intentions on others will often lead to their corruption. This is not in accordance with the wishes of God or Buddha, either.

While the evil form of communism makes everybody equally poor, today, the evil form of "liberalism" is trying to make us believe in the illusion that it is creating a wealthy communist society. However, if what these politicians are doing through using their power is, in the free market economy of a capitalist society, to easily deprive those who are making an effort, racking their brains and perspiring, of their assets and redistributing those assets to those who have not made any effort, thereby increasing the number of people who choose not to work, then unfortunately, this goes against acts of mercy and will end up leading people in the direction of corruption.

There is more than just a merciful aspect to God. Never forget that God also expects you to do what you can do; walk and run on your own two feet, carry heavy bags on your own back, study on your own, till the land on your own and catch fish for yourself.

7

The Relationship between Self-Power And Outside Power, as Taught by The Light of Asia

UDA:

We have learned that, as the children of God or Buddha, we all have to make efforts on the basis of the spirit of self-help. This is a simple but very important teaching, and I think very few religious leaders in the past have taught this principle so clearly. This is different from the teaching of Jesus or Muhammad.

People in general tend to think superficially that religions only teach the importance of an outside power, but as you have just taught us, I think self-help is a basic attitude for humans. In this sense, I believe that there is a pressing need to convey this lofty idea to the people of the world, and I am deeply convinced that this is a teaching that can save people who live in every corner of the globe. And we are now determined to spread with all our might the truth that the Savior has been born in Japan to bring salvation to all people of the world.

Lastly, I would like to ask you a little daring question. During this session of over an hour, you have taught us the importance of self-help spirit and showed us the profound Truth that encompasses lofty political philosophy. We have already had a guess at who you are, but we would appreciate it if you could tell us who exactly you, the guardian spirit of Master Ryuho Okawa, are.

OKAWA'S GUARDIAN SPIRIT:

Before I answer your question, I would like to add one more thing to what you have just said. I said that the spirit of self-help is important, but I'm not denying outside power altogether. If there was only the teaching on the spirit of self-help, then it is possible that it would give rise to people with no faith. This must be noted.

You must never forget that the teaching of self-help must not lead you to lose your faith; it does not encourage you to live in this world solely on the basis of your worldly abilities or talents. Although I believe that self-help needs to be the 70 or 80 percent, you also need to have faith in an outside power and believe that the power of God or Buddha, and the power of angels and Bodhisattvas, are at work.

But this concept of an outside power must not be replaced by thoughts of relying solely on others, for example, "The government will take care of everything for us," or "Those who have achieved great success in business should pay all the costs of social welfare." I want to emphasize that this kind of replacement of thoughts is wrong. You need to understand this relationship between self-power and outside power.

Only one person could teach this Truth in the past. He was called "the Light of Asia," and I believe all Happy Science believers should know who that is.

UDA:
Thank you very much.

SATOMURA:
Gautama Buddha, thank you very much.

8

His Disciples, Go on Turning The Wheel of Dharma!

Make efforts with a stronger sense of mission

SATOMURA:

This is the last question and I want to hear your words again. Please tell us about the mission of Master Ryuho Okawa in this era, and the mission of the Happy Science Group that he has founded.

OKAWA'S GUARDIAN SPIRIT:

In the next era, his disciples must turn the wheel of Dharma. You are required to make efforts while having stronger awareness.

The first wheel of Dharma had already started to turn, then the next wheel started turning, then the next, and many wheels are turning. To spread this Truth all over the world, I desire that every disciple becomes an Angel of Light, emitting light and further building up his or her efforts.

You must be strong.

Never give in to materialism, nor be defeated by the abusive words of the mass media.

Also, never be deluded by the words of those who do not have firm belief in our faith and complain that their hunger for fame, desire for power, greed for money and other things weren't satisfied sufficiently. I want to say these things in the end.

SATOMURA:

Thank you very much. With the determination to die for the Truth, we, disciples will make efforts and strive hard to turn the wheel of Dharma, as it gets bigger and bigger.

OKAWA'S GUARDIAN SPIRIT:

Good.

SATOMURA:

Gautama Buddha, Shakyamuni Buddha, thank you indeed.

RYUHO OKAWA:

[*To his guardian spirit*] Thank you very much.

I want to walk wholeheartedly
This long path of diligent efforts

RYUHO OKAWA:

That's it. A thousand years is like a day. He does not seem to mind whether we have achieved something or not at the deadline of each worldly event. He meant that humans on earth should all undergo soul training through each challenge. This is true of my disciples, as well as people outside our group.

Our principle Laws for next year [*2014*] will be *The Laws of Perseverance*. This makes me feel like hardships are coming my way, but we want to walk steadily the path of diligent efforts.

SATOMURA:

Thank you very much for this great opportunity today.

RYUHO OKAWA:

You're welcome.

Afterword

Since the end of World War II, it has been regarded as wrong for a religion to intervene in politics or exercise political power. This is because people believe that Japan was defeated in the last war as a result of the strong backing by State Shinto. However, the fundamental philosophy supporting the constitutional democracy based on the current Japanese Constitution is very weak. If you think of the constitution as simply the fruits of research into the system from the standpoint of social sciences, then I must say that your insight is shallow.

If we trace back the constitutions and legislation of Western countries, we can find their source in the Ten Commandments that Moses received from God over 3,000 years ago. Over 2,500 years ago, Shakyamuni Buddha also taught the Five Precepts* and the Ten Good Deeds†. These do not necessarily carry any punishment, but indicate the direction in which Buddhist believers should aim of their own accord in their spiritual training. Being born as a prince of the Shakya clan, Shakyamuni Buddha, too, was brought up to be a political ruler but later became a religious leader instead. He interceded

---

* Five precepts in traditional Buddhism that followers should keep: do not kill, do not steal, do not engage in improper sexual conduct, do not make false statements, and do not drink alcohol.

† The 10 precepts of Mahayana Buddhism that followers should keep: do not kill, do not steal, do not indulge in sexual misconduct, do not lie, do not use double-tongued speech, do not use abusive speech, do not use irresponsible speech, no greed, no hatred, and no delusion.

between the Magadha and Kosala kingdoms, and served as a political adviser to the King of Magadha [the strongest of the 16 Indian states at that time]. He was rational, logical, philosophical and well versed in real politics. No further explanation should be necessary.

July 13, 2013
Master and CEO of the Happy Science Group
Ryuho Okawa

ABOUT THE AUTHOR

Founder and CEO of Happy Science Group.

Ryuho Okawa was born on July 7th 1956, in Tokushima, Japan. After graduating from the University of Tokyo with a law degree, he joined a Tokyo-based trading house. While working at its New York headquarters, he studied international finance at the Graduate Center of the City University of New York. In 1981, he attained Great Enlightenment and became aware that he is El Cantare with a mission to bring salvation to all humankind.

In 1986, he established Happy Science. It now has members in over 165 countries across the world, with more than 700 branches and temples as well as 10,000 missionary houses around the world.

He has given over 3,450 lectures (of which more than 150 are in English) and published over 3,000 books (of which more than 600 are Spiritual Interview Series), and many are translated into 40 languages. Along with *The Laws of the Sun* and *The Laws Of Messiah*, many of the books have become best sellers or million sellers. To date, Happy Science has produced 25 movies. The original story and original concept were given by the Executive Producer Ryuho Okawa. He has also composed music and written lyrics of over 450 pieces.

Moreover, he is the Founder of Happy Science University and Happy Science Academy (Junior and Senior High School), Founder and President of the Happiness Realization Party, Founder and Honorary Headmaster of Happy Science Institute of Government and Management, Founder of IRH Press Co., Ltd., and the Chairperson of NEW STAR PRODUCTION Co., Ltd. and ARI Production Co., Ltd.

WHAT IS EL CANTARE?

El Cantare means "the Light of the Earth," and is the Supreme God of the Earth who has been guiding humankind since the beginning of Genesis. He is whom Jesus called Father and Muhammad called Allah, and is *Ame-no-Mioya-Gami*, Japanese Father God. Different parts of El Cantare's core consciousness have descended to Earth in the past, once as Alpha and another as Elohim. His branch spirits, such as Shakyamuni Buddha and Hermes, have descended to Earth many times and helped to flourish many civilizations. To unite various religions and to integrate various fields of study in order to build a new civilization on Earth, a part of the core consciousness has descended to Earth as Master Ryuho Okawa.

Alpha is a part of the core consciousness of El Cantare who descended to Earth around 330 million years ago. Alpha preached Earth's Truths to harmonize and unify Earth-born humans and space people who came from other planets.

Elohim is a part of El Cantare's core consciousness who descended to Earth around 150 million years ago. He gave wisdom, mainly on the differences of light and darkness, good and evil.

Ame-no-Mioya-Gami (Japanese Father God) is the Creator God and the Father God who appears in the ancient literature, *Hotsuma Tsutae*. It is believed that He descended on the foothills of Mt. Fuji about 30,000 years ago and built the Fuji dynasty, which is the root of the Japanese civilization. With justice as the central pillar, Ame-no-Mioya-Gami's teachings spread to ancient civilizations of other countries in the world.

Shakyamuni Buddha was born as a prince into the Shakya Clan in India around 2,600 years ago. When he was 29 years old, he renounced the world and sought enlightenment. He later attained Great Enlightenment and founded Buddhism.

Hermes is one of the 12 Olympian gods in Greek mythology, but the spiritual Truth is that he taught the teachings of love and progress around 4,300 years ago that became the origin of the current Western civilization. He is a hero that truly existed.

Ophealis was born in Greece around 6,500 years ago and was the leader who took an expedition to as far as Egypt. He is the God of miracles, prosperity, and arts, and is known as Osiris in the Egyptian mythology.

Rient Arl Croud was born as a king of the ancient Incan Empire around 7,000 years ago and taught about the mysteries of the mind. In the heavenly world, he is responsible for the interactions that take place between various planets.

Thoth was an almighty leader who built the golden age of the Atlantic civilization around 12,000 years ago. In the Egyptian mythology, he is known as god Thoth.

Ra Mu was a leader who built the golden age of the civilization of Mu around 17,000 years ago. As a religious leader and a politician, he ruled by uniting religion and politics.

ABOUT HAPPY SCIENCE

Happy Science is a global movement that empowers individuals to find purpose and spiritual happiness and to share that happiness with their families, societies, and the world. With more than 12 million members around the world, Happy Science aims to increase awareness of spiritual truths and expand our capacity for love, compassion, and joy so that together we can create the kind of world we all wish to live in.

Activities at Happy Science are based on the Principle of Happiness (Love, Wisdom, Self-Reflection, and Progress). This principle embraces worldwide philosophies and beliefs, transcending boundaries of culture and religions.

Love teaches us to give ourselves freely without expecting anything in return; it encompasses giving, nurturing, and forgiving.

Wisdom leads us to the insights of spiritual truths, and opens us to the true meaning of life and the will of God (the universe, the highest power, Buddha).

Self-Reflection brings a mindful, nonjudgmental lens to our thoughts and actions to help us find our truest selves—the essence of our souls—and deepen our connection to the highest power. It helps us attain a clean and peaceful mind and leads us to the right life path.

Progress emphasizes the positive, dynamic aspects of our spiritual growth—actions we can take to manifest and spread happiness around the world. It's a path that not only expands our soul growth, but also furthers the collective potential of the world we live in.

PROGRAMS AND EVENTS

The doors of Happy Science are open to all. We offer a variety of programs and events, including self-exploration and self-growth programs, spiritual seminars, meditation and contemplation sessions, study groups, and book events.

Our programs are designed to:
* Deepen your understanding of your purpose and meaning in life
* Improve your relationships and increase your capacity to love unconditionally
* Attain peace of mind, decrease anxiety and stress, and feel positive
* Gain deeper insights and a broader perspective on the world
* Learn how to overcome life's challenges
   ... and much more.

For more information, visit hoppy-science.org.

OUR ACTIVITIES

Happy Science does other various activities to provide support for those in need.

◆ **You Are An Angel! General Incorporated Association**

Happy Science has a volunteer network in Japan that encourages and supports children with disabilities as well as their parents and guardians.

◆ **Never Mind School for Truancy**

At 'Never Mind,' we support students who find it very challenging to attend schools in Japan. We also nurture their self-help spirit and power to rebound against obstacles in life based on Master Okawa's teachings and faith.

◆ **"Prevention Against Suicide" Campaign since 2003**

A nationwide campaign to reduce suicides; over 20,000 people commit suicide every year in Japan. "The Suicide Prevention Website-Words of Truth for You-" presents spiritual prescriptions for worries such as depression, lost love, extramarital affairs, bullying and work-related problems, thereby saving many lives.

◆ **Support for Anti-bullying Campaigns**

Happy Science provides support for a group of parents and guardians, Network to Protect Children from Bullying, a general incorporated foundation launched in Japan to end bullying, including those that can even be called a criminal offense. So far, the network received more than 5,000 cases and resolved 90% of them.

- **The Golden Age Scholarship**

  This scholarship is granted to students who can contribute greatly and bring a hopeful future to the world.

- **Success No.1**

  Buddha's Truth Afterschool Academy

  Happy Science has over 180 classrooms throughout Japan and in several cities around the world that focus on afterschool education for children. The education focuses on faith and morals in addition to supporting children's school studies.

- **Angel Plan V**

  For children under the age of kindergarten, Happy Science holds classes for nurturing healthy, positive, and creative boys and girls.

- **Future Stars Training Department**

  The Future Stars Training Department was founded within the Happy Science Media Division with the goal of nurturing talented individuals to become successful in the performing arts and entertainment industry.

- **NEW STAR PRODUCTION Co., Ltd.**

  ARI Production Co., Ltd.

  We have companies to nurture actors and actresses, artists, and vocalists. They are also involved in film production.

CONTACT INFORMATION

Happy Science is a worldwide organization with branches and temples around the globe. For a comprehensive list, visit the worldwide directory at *happy-science.org*. The following are some of the many Happy Science locations:

UNITED STATES AND CANADA

New York
79 Franklin St., New York, NY 10013, USA
Phone: 1-212-343-7972
Fax: 1-212-343-7973
Email: ny@happy-science.org
Website: happyscience-usa.org

New Jersey
66 Hudson St., #2R, Hoboken, NJ 07030, USA
Phone: 1-201-313-0127
Email: nj@happy-science.org
Website: happyscience-usa.org

Chicago
2300 Barrington Rd., Suite #400,
Hoffman Estates, IL 60169, USA
Phone: 1-630-937-3077
Email: chicago@happy-science.org
Website: happyscience-usa.org

Florida
5208 8th St., Zephyrhills, FL 33542, USA
Phone: 1-813-715-0000
Fax: 1-813-715-0010
Email: florida@happy-science.org
Website: happyscience-usa.org

Atlanta
1874 Piedmont Ave., NE Suite 360-C
Atlanta, GA 30324, USA
Phone: 1-404-892-7770
Email: atlanta@happy-science.org
Website: happyscience-usa.org

San Francisco
525 Clinton St.
Redwood City, CA 94062, USA
Phone & Fax: 1-650-363-2777
Email: sf@happy-science.org
Website: happyscience-usa.org

Los Angeles
1590 E. Del Mar Blvd., Pasadena, CA 91106, USA
Phone: 1-626-395-7775
Fax: 1-626-395-7776
Email: la@happy-science.org
Website: happyscience-usa.org

Orange County
16541 Gothard St. Suite 104
Huntington Beach, CA 92647
Phone: 1-714-659-1501
Email: oc@happy-science.org
Website: happyscience-usa.org

San Diego
7841 Balboa Ave. Suite #202
San Diego, CA 92111, USA
Phone: 1-626-395-7775
Fax: 1-626-395-7776
E-mail: sandiego@happy-science.org
Website: happyscience-usa.org

Hawaii
Phone: 1-808-591-9772
Fax: 1-808-591-9776
Email: hi@happy-science.org
Website: happyscience-usa.org

Kauai
3343 Kanakolu Street, Suite 5
Lihue, HI 96766, USA
Phone: 1-808-822-7007
Fax: 1-808-822-6007
Email: kauai-hi@happy-science.org
Website: happyscience-usa.org

Toronto

845 The Queensway
Etobicoke, ON M8Z 1N6, Canada
Phone: 1-416-901-3747
Email: toronto@happy-science.org
Website: happy-science.ca

Vancouver

#201-2607 East 49th Avenue,
Vancouver, BC, V5S 1J9, Canada
Phone: 1-604-437-7735
Fax: 1-604-437-7764
Email: vancouver@happy-science.org
Website: happy-science.ca

INTERNATIONAL

Tokyo

1-6-7 Togoshi, Shinagawa,
Tokyo, 142-0041, Japan
Phone: 81-3-6384-5770
Fax: 81-3-6384-5776
Email: tokyo@happy-science.org
Website: happy-science.org

Seoul

74, Sadang-ro 27-gil,
Dongjak-gu, Seoul, Korea
Phone: 82-2-3478-8777
Fax: 82-2-3478-9777
Email: korea@happy-science.org
Website: happyscience-korea.org

London

3 Margaret St.
London, W1W 8RE United Kingdom
Phone: 44-20-7323-9255
Fax: 44-20-7323-9344
Email: eu@happy-science.org
Website: www.happyscience-uk.org

Taipei

No. 89, Lane 155, Dunhua N. Road,
Songshan District, Taipei City 105, Taiwan
Phone: 886-2-2719-9377
Fax: 886-2-2719-5570
Email: taiwan@happy-science.org
Website: happyscience-tw.org

Sydney

516 Pacific Highway, Lane Cove North,
2066 NSW, Australia
Phone: 61-2-9411-2877
Fax: 61-2-9411-2822
Email: sydney@happy-science.org

Kuala Lumpur

No 22A, Block 2, Jalil Link Jalan Jalil
Jaya 2, Bukit Jalil 57000,
Kuala Lumpur, Malaysia
Phone: 60-3-8998-7877
Fax: 60-3-8998-7977
Email: malaysia@happy-science.org
Website: happyscience.org.my

Sao Paulo

Rua. Domingos de Morais 1154,
Vila Mariana, Sao Paulo SP
CEP 04010-100, Brazil
Phone: 55-11-5088-3800
Email: sp@happy-science.org
Website: happyscience.com.br

Kathmandu

Kathmandu Metropolitan City,
Ward No. 15, Ring Road, Kimdol,
Sitapaila Kathmandu, Nepal
Phone: 977-1-427-2931
Email: nepal@happy-science.org

Jundiai

Rua Congo, 447, Jd. Bonfiglioli
Jundiai-CEP, 13207-340, Brazil
Phone: 55-11-4587-5952
Email: jundiai@happy-science.org

Kampala

Plot 877 Ruhaga Road, Kampala
P.O. Box 34130 Kampala, UGANDA
Phone: 256-79-4682-121
Email: uganda@happy-science.org

ABOUT HAPPINESS REALIZATION PARTY

The Happiness Realization Party (HRP) was founded in May 2009 by Master Ryuho Okawa as part of the Happy Science Group. HRP strives to improve the Japanese society, based on three basic political principles of "freedom, democracy, and faith," and let Japan promote individual and public happiness from Asia to the world as a leader nation.

1) Diplomacy and Security: Protecting Freedom, Democracy, and Faith of Japan and the World from China's Totalitarianism

Japan's current defense system is insufficient against China's expanding hegemony and the threat of North Korea's nuclear missiles. Japan, as the leader of Asia, must strengthen its defense power and promote strategic diplomacy together with the nations which share the values of freedom, democracy, and faith. Further, HRP aims to realize world peace under the leadership of Japan, the nation with the spirit of religious tolerance.

2) Economy: Early economic recovery through utilizing the "wisdom of the private sector"

Economy has been damaged severely by the novel coronavirus originated in China. Many companies have been forced into bankruptcy or out of business. What is needed for economic recovery now is not subsidies and regulations by the government, but policies which can utilize the "wisdom of the private sector."

For more information, visit en.hr-party.jp

ABOUT HS PRESS

HS Press is an imprint of IRH Press Co., Ltd. IRH Press Co., Ltd., based in Tokyo, was founded in 1987 as a publishing division of Happy Science. IRH Press publishes religious and spiritual books, journals, magazines and also operates broadcast and film production enterprises. For more information, visit *okawabooks.com*.

Follow us on:

f Facebook: Okawa Books   Instagram: OkawaBooks
Youtube: Okawa Books   Twitter: Okawa Books
Pinterest: Okawa Books   Goodreads: Ryuho Okawa

NEWSLETTER

To receive book related news, promotions and events, please subscribe to our newsletter below.

eepurl.com/bsMeJj

AUDIO / VISUAL MEDIA

YOUTUBE

PODCAST

Introduction of Ryuho Okawa's titles; topics ranging from self-help, current affairs, spirituality, religion, and the universe.

BOOKS BY RYUHO OKAWA

THE LAWS OF THE SUN
One Source, One Planet, One People

ISBN: 978-1-942125-43-3

$15.95 (Paperback)

IMAGINE IF YOU COULD ASK GOD why He created this world and what spiritual laws He used to shape us—and everything around us. If we could understand His designs and intentions, we could discover what our goals in life should be and whether our actions move us closer to those goals or farther away.

At a young age, a spiritual calling prompted Ryuho Okawa to outline what he innately understood to be universal truths for all humankind. In *The Laws of the Sun*, Okawa outlines these laws of the universe and provides a road map for living one's life with greater purpose and meaning.

In this powerful book, Ryuho Okawa reveals the transcendent nature of consciousness and the secrets of our multidimensional universe and our place in it. By understanding the different stages of love and following the Buddhist Eightfold Path, he believes we can speed up our eternal process of development. *The Laws of the Sun* shows the way to realize true happiness—a happiness that continues from this world through the other.

CHANGE YOUR LIFE, CHANGE THE WORLD

A SPIRITUAL GUIDE TO LIVING NOW

ISBN: 978-0-9826985-0-1

$16.95 (Paperback)

MASTER RYUHO OKAWA calls out to people of all nations to remember their true spiritual roots and to build our planet into a united Earth of peace, prosperity, and happiness. With the spiritual wisdom contained in this book, each and every one of us can change our lives and change the world.

"To save the seven billion people on Earth, God has countless angels working constantly, every day, on His behalf." —Chapter 3

THE MOMENT OF TRUTH

BECOME A LIVING ANGEL TODAY

ISBN: 978-0-9826985-7-0

$14.95 (Paperback)

MASTER OKAWA shows that we are essentially spiritual beings and that our true and lasting happiness is not found within the material world but rather in acts of unconditional and selfless love toward the greater world. These pages reveal God's mind, His mercy, and His hope that many of us will become living angels that shine light onto this world.

THE NINE DIMENSIONS

UNVEILING THE LAWS OF ETERNITY

ISBN: 978-0-9826985-6-3

$15.95 (Paperback)

THIS BOOK IS YOUR GATE TO HEAVEN. In this book, Master Okawa shows that God designed this world and the vast, wondrous world of our afterlife as a school with many levels through which our souls learn and grow. This book is a window into the mind of our loving God, who encourages us to grow into greater angels.

SECRETS OF
THE EVERLASTING TRUTHS

A NEW PARADIGM FOR LIVING ON EARTH

ISBN: 978-1-937673-10-9

$14.95 (Paperback)

OUR BELIEF IN THE INVISIBLE IS OUR FUTURE. It is our knowledge about the everlasting spiritual laws and our belief in the invisible that will make it possible for us to solve the world's problems and bring our entire planet together. When you discover the secrets in this book, your view of yourself and the world will be changed dramatically and forever.

THE LAWS OF PERSEVERANCE
REVERSING YOUR COMMON SENSE

ISBN: 978-1-937673-56-7

$14.95 (Paperback)

"No matter how much you suffer, the Truth will gradually shine forth as you continue to endure hardships. Therefore, simply strengthen your mind and keep making constant efforts in times of endurance, however ordinary they may be.

Eventually, you will come out of your slump and overcome your hardships. And, as you try and aim to reverse the common sense, you will one day understand that people can be "undefeated" even if they seem to have lost in this world. In that process, you may sometimes feel that virtue is being generated."

—From Postscript

THINK BIG!

BE POSITIVE AND BE BRAVE TO ACHIEVE YOUR DREAMS

ISBN: 978-1-942125-04-4

$12.95 (Paperback)

In *Think Big* Master Ryuho Okawa shares his own philosophy of thinking big, thinking positive, and being brave for they are essential mindsets in achieving our dreams. While there is an especial emphasis on developing this philosophy while we're young, it is universal and valuable for people of all ages and all walks of life who want to achieve their dreams and live a successful life. If you do not have any dreams yet, then this is a must-have book for discovering why having ideals are an essential part of life. If you already have aspirations, then discover how to make them come true. If you are in college, find out valuable tips on how to get a head start on developing the think big mindset.

ALSO BY RYUHO OKAWA

THE TEN PRINCIPLES FROM EL CANTARE VOLUME I
Ryuho Okawa's First Lectures on His Basic Teachings

THE TEN PRINCIPLES FROM EL CANTARE VOLUME II
Ryuho Okawa's First Lectures on His Wish to Save the World

THE GOLDEN LAWS
History through the Eyes of the Eternal Buddha

THE STARTING POINT OF HAPPINESS
A Practical and Intuitive Guide to Discovering Love, Wisdom, and Faith

LOVE, NURTURE, AND FORGIVE
A Handbook to Add a New Richness to Your Life

AN UNSHAKABLE MIND
How to Overcome Life's Difficulties

THE ORIGIN OF LOVE
On the Beauty of Compassion

INVINCIBLE THINKING
An Essential Guide for a Lifetime of Growth, Success, and Triumph

GUIDEPOSTS TO HAPPINESS
Prescriptions for a Wonderful Life

THE LAWS OF HAPPINESS
Love, Wisdom, Self-Reflection and Progress

TIPS TO FIND HAPPINESS
Creating a Harmonious Home for Your Spouse, Your Children, and Yourself

THE PHILOSOPHY OF PROGRESS
Higher Thinking for Developing Infinite Prosperity

THE ESSENCE OF BUDDHA
The Path to Enlightenment

THE CHALLENGE OF THE MIND
An Essential Guide to Buddha's Teachings:
Zen, Karma, and Enlightenment

THE CHALLENGE OF ENLIGHTENMENT
Realize Your Inner Potential

THE MANIFESTO OF THE HAPPINESS
REALIZATION PARTY

RYUHO OKAWA: A POLITICAL REVOLUTIONARY
The Originator of Abenomics and Father of the Happiness Realization Party

HIGHER EDUCATION SERIES

THE NEW IDEA OF A UNIVERSITY
The Groundbreaking Mission of Happy Science University

THE BASIC TEACHINGS OF HAPPY SCIENCE
A Happiness Theory on Truth and Faith

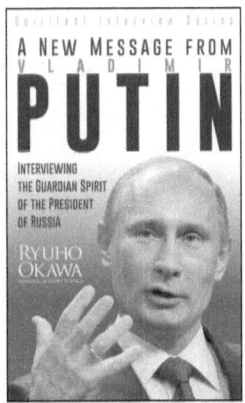

A NEW MESSAGE FROM VLADIMIR PUTIN

INTERVIEWING THE GUARDIAN SPIRIT OF THE PRESIDENT OF RUSSIA

ISBN: 978-1-937673-94-9

$14.95 (Paperback)

We hereby bring you the most recent spiritual message from the guardian spirit of President Putin, the politician who is the center of attention of not just the people of Russia but of the whole world, regardless of it being in a good or a bad way. In the Preface, it says, "President Putin's true intentions, which are 90 percent misunderstood."

We hope that, through this book, the reader will come to understand the true thoughts of Mr. Putin which are still undisclosed to the public. And, we hope that the reader will foresee the new world order that this skilled politician is thinking of, and make use of that in predicting how the international affairs will turn out in the future.

THE SECRET BEHIND
"THE RAPE OF NANKING"

A Spiritual Confession by Iris Chang

ISBN: 978-1-941779-08-8

$9.95 (Paperback)

Sometimes a single book can determine how the international society sees history, as well as give a great impact on international relations. If a fabricated history had spread throughout the world and is subjecting the citizens of a particular country to humiliation that they don't deserve, then speaking from international justice and humanitarian viewpoints, such history must be rewritten in an objective and impartial manner. There is a phrase, "History is written by the victors." The usual process is that, after a war, the victors come up with a one-sided historical view that is advantageous to them and historical researchers of later generations gradually make corrections to it.

Nevertheless, sometimes history takes a sudden turn due to revelations from Heaven. This book is a rare example of that. The author of a book which gave a great impact on the historical view that had spread throughout the international society today confessed the truth regarding the content of her book and its background, just 10 years after her death, in a form of a spiritual message.

THE GENIUS OF ICHIRO

The Secret Behind His Four Thousand Hits

ISBN: 978-1-941779-04-0

$14.95 (Paperback)

Ichiro Suzuki arrived in Seattle in 2001 as a mostly anonymous free agent from Japan's NPB, and while there was buzz about his potential, no one really knew what to expect. Since then, he has set many records in American Major League Baseball, including the record for most hits in a single season (262) and longest streak of two-hundred-hit seasons (ten years). On August 21, 2013, he got the four thousandth hit of his professional baseball career. This spiritual interview reveals the "making of Ichiro," including the secrets to his professionalism, his techniques for overcoming slumps, and how he made it to the top. The interview highlights Ichiro's unique traits that continue to impress us, twelve years after he first unleashed the laser beam.

ON HAPPINESS REVOLUTION

A SPIRITUAL INTERVIEW WITH HANNAH ARENDT

ISBN: 978-1-937673-82-6

$14.95 (Paperback)

Since 2010, Master Ryuho Okawa has published over two hundred spiritual messages, in Japanese, from the spirits of historical men and women and the guardian spirits of today's living figures. With this Spiritual Interview Series, Master Okawa is now making these important messages available in English. The books in this series are messages from the spirits or guardian spirits of people who have a great deal of influence over world affairs. These messages reveal these powerful figures' hidden intentions and disclose facts that even news reporters would have difficulty drawing out. Master Okawa's in-depth analyses of these messages give us the tools that we need to understand and confront the dangers that lie ahead of us. Master Okawa hopes to show readers that the spirit world and spirits are real, and that by understanding spiritual truths, we can bring a peaceful end to international conflicts and create solutions to a variety of global crises.

ARE ISLAMIC EXTREMISTS JIHADISTS OR TERRORISTS?
THE NECESSITY OF FREEDOM IN ISLAMIC COUNTRIES

ISBN: 978-1-941779-14-9

$14.95 (Paperback)

The West has been leading a long war on terror since the 9/11 terrorist attacks in 2001 on American soil by Osama bin Laden's al-Qaeda. Even after the assassination of Osama bin Laden on May 2, 2011, by President Obama's Special Forces unit, terrorist attacks have continued around the world. On January 16, 2013, an international crisis erupted when Islamic terrorists organized by Mokhtar Belmokhtar lay siege to an Algerian gas plant. After the Algerian government sent in a special forces unit, thirty-nine foreign hostages were killed and 685 Algerian workers and one hundred foreigners escaped or were freed. *

Are the attacks by Islamic extremist groups like al-Qaeda and the organization led by Mokhtar Belmokhtar unjust acts of terror? Or are they justified acts of a holy war, as the self-proclaimed jihadists claim? In this interview with Osama bin Laden, Master Ryuho Okawa provides us with his conclusive answer to these questions.

* "Q&A: Hostage Crisis in Algeria," BBC News, January 21, 2013, http://www.bbc.com/news/world-africa-21056884.

LEADERSHIP SECRETS OF LIU BANG

THE EMPEROR OF CHINA'S HAN DYNASTY
WITH A SURPRISING CONNECTION WITH STEVEN SPIELBERG

ISBN: 978-1-941779-17-0

$14.95 (Paperback)

Liu Bang, also known as Gaozu, began from humble peasant roots and served as a police officer under the Qin dynasty. He rose through the ranks, first receiving control of western China, and eventually becoming the ruler of China as the founder and first emperor of the Han dynasty (206 BCE–220 CE). The histories of kings and rulers often provide valuable lessons about the universal principles that can be applied to today's management, entrepreneurship, and all types of large undertakings. As this spiritual interview has shown, Liu Bang's strengths and achievements are marked by a strong global element. Everyone who aspires to lead a large organization can learn from his ability to win people's hearts. You may be surprised to discover that this long-ago emperor of China is living today in the United States as one of the world's most famous film directors, Steven Spielberg.

THE TRUTH OF NANKING AND COMFORT WOMEN ISSUES

A Spiritual Reading into World War II
by Edgar Cayce

ISBN: 978-1-937673-86-4

$14.95 (Paperback)

Did the so-called "Nanking Massacre" and the military comfort women forcefully taken by the Japanese troops actually exist as historical facts? In this book, we attempt to investigate whether the two events actually took place by using a new method. This is not merely to restore the international honor of Japan. We are hoping to review the causes of World War II, look over the world justice made by the victorious nations after the war and reveal the true world history.

THE NEW DIPLOMATIC STRATEGIES OF SIR WINSTON CHURCHILL

A SPIRITUAL INTERVIEW WITH THE FORMER PRIME MINISTER REGARDING THE AGE OF PERSEVERANCE

ISBN: 978-1-937673-85-7

$14.95 (Paperback)

Today, two politicians are criticized and compared to Hitler; President Vladimir Putin of Russia and Prime Minister Shinzo Abe of Japan. Are these politicians really dangerous to be likened to Hitler? Or, just like in Hitler's case, can it be that another truly dangerous politician exists in another country that is yet to be discovered? If there is a chance to hear the opinion of Sir Winston Churchill, considered to be Hitler's arch enemy, journalists around the world would probably be interested to hear this.

The series on Spiritual Messages by Ryuho Okawa, Happy Science, made this possible. This book contains a record of an interview conducted with the spirit of former British Prime Minister Churchill by Master Okawa in March this year. It is a record of an interview on issues related to the "next appearance of Hitler," and on current international affairs.

THE ART OF BUSINESS REVITALIZATION

MANAGEMENT WISDOM FROM JACK WELCH, CARLOS GHOSN, AND BILL GATES

ISBN: 978-1-937673-70-3

$19.95 (Paperback)

In *The Art of Business Revitalization: Management Wisdom from Jack Welch*, Carlos Ghosn, and Bill Gates, Master Ryuho Okawa conducts spiritual interviews with three of the greatest executives of our time. General Electric's Jack Welch, Renault and Nissan's Carlos Ghosn, and Microsoft's Bill Gates give readers a glimpse into how they took hold of opportunities and turned them into successes. What management philosophies helped Jack Welch and Carlos Ghosn turn around their companies during downturns? What is Bill Gates's secret to creating products that become global standards? What human resources management and education philosophies have they drawn upon to keep their companies at the top? This book reveals the secrets to their achievements.

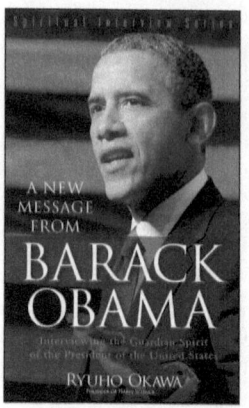

A NEW MESSAGE FROM
BARACK OBAMA

INTERVIEWING THE GUARDIAN SPIRIT OF
THE PRESIDENT OF THE UNITED STATES

ISBN: 978-1-937673-89-5

$14.95 (Paperback)

In April 2014, President Obama embarked on his fifth trip to Asia during his time in office to discuss the pressing issues in the Asia-pacific region. A week before his Asia trip, Master Ryuho Okawa held a spiritual interview with Barack Obama, which revealed his true objectives of his Asia tour and about his thoughts on current affairs in the world. What is President Obama's vision of America's role in the world today? Why does he believe that America is not the world's policeman? This spiritual interview reveals President Obama's stance on international relations including America's relationship with China, the Ukraine crisis and Islamic extremism. It also discloses his honest feelings about Japanese Prime Minister Abe and Russian President Putin. Now that America is "on the verge of crisis," as the guardian spirit of President Obama says in this interview, we all need to think about how we can achieve security, justice and peace in the world without the "world's policeman."

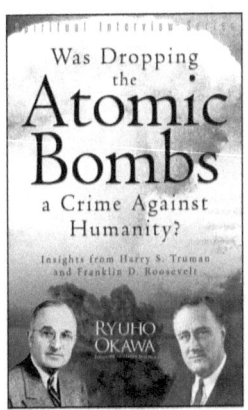

WAS DROPPING THE ATOMIC BOMBS A CRIME AGAINST HUMANITY?

INSIGHTS FROM HARRY S. TRUMAN
AND FRANKLIN D. ROOSEVELT

ISBN: 978-1-937673-78-9

$14.95 (Paperback)

Was there any true justification for the atomic bombing of Hiroshima and Nagasaki? To answer to this question, Master Ryuho Okawa conducted spiritual interviews with Harry S. Truman and Franklin D. Roosevelt, the two presidents who presided over the United States' participation in World War II. Could anything justify the use of nuclear weapons on civilians? Was Pearl Harbor really a sneak attack, or did Franklin Roosevelt know of it beforehand? This book reveals valuable information that will help the world gain a truthful understanding of world history.

JAPAN! REGAIN YOUR SAMURAI SPIRIT

A Message from the Guardian Spirit of Lee Teng-hui, Former President of the Republic of China

IISBN: 978-1-937673-77-2

$14.95 (Paperback)

This book is the record of interviews conducted on Former President of Taiwan Lee Teng-hui's subconscious [guardian spirit] in February 2014. His true thoughts, as well as the truth on modern East-Asian history, were revealed in these interviews. The book is filled with hints on how to give another thought to the causes of World War II. As it is stated in the afterword, this is a book which we want "all politicians, all people in the media, and everyone who talks about politics" to read.

DIPLOMATIC STRATEGY
FOR JAPAN, U.S. AND CHINA

A MESSAGE FROM THE GUARDIAN SPIRIT OF
DIPLOMATIC ANALYST HISAHIKO OKAZAKI

ISBN: 978-1-937673-75-8

$14.95 (Paperback)

This book contains the interview conducted with the guardian spirit of former diplomat, Hisahiko Okazaki, a conservative commentator representative to Japan. An astonishing relation between Admiral Perry and Okazaki is revealed in this interview. By reading this book, you will come to know what Admiral Perry thinks on the current situation of the world, and the relation between Japan and the United States, 160 years later since he opened up Japan which was in seclusion.

WHY I AM ANTI-JAPAN

INTERVIEWING THE GUARDIAN SPIRIT OF
KOREAN PRESIDENT PARK GEUN-HYE

ISBN: 978-1-937673-67-3

$14.95 (Paperback)

This book is the record of interviews conducted on President Park's subconscious [guardian spirit] in February 2014, which were done in order to find out the fundamental reason to her anti-Japanese sentiments. Her true thoughts, as well as the truth on modern Japan-Korea history, were revealed in these interviews. By having numerous people in the world know of this truth, starting with the Japanese, South Koreans, Americans and the Chinese, the path to create a constructive future of the Pacific Basin should open as we resolve the conflicting emotions between Japan and South Korea in the international society.

A WARNING TO
SOUTH KOREA'S PRESIDENT

WORDS FROM HER FATHER,
FORMER PRESIDENT PARK CHUNG-HEE

ISBN: 978-1-937673-65-9

$14.95 (Paperback)

Park Chung-hee served as the president of the Republic of Korea (South Korea) for almost sixteen years, from 1963 until his death in 1979. Today, people around the world know him as the assassinated father of Park Geun-hye, the current and first female president of South Korea. In this spiritual interview, Park Chung-hee's spirit shares his opinions on the roles of South Korea, Japan, the United States, China, and North Korea in the global context. What are his thoughts on the Takeshima island dispute, the comfort-women issue, China's future prospects, and the direction South Korea should take as a country? A Warning to South Korea's President is a father's message to his daughter as he seeks to guide their nation in the right direction. This interview lets us see history in a new light and shows us how to build a better future for the Asia-Pacific region.

INTERVIEWING THE GUARDIAN SPIRIT OF U.S. AMBASSADOR CAROLINE KENNEDY
A NEW BRIDGE BETWEEN JAPAN AND THE U.S.

ISBN: 978-1-937673-63-5

$14.95 (Paperback)

CONTENTS

FOR THE FUTURE OF
THAILAND AND JAPAN

INTERVIEWING THE GUARDIAN SPIRIT OF
YINGLUCK SHINAWATRA

ISBN: 978-1-937673-59-8

$14.95 (Paperback)

In December 2013, Thailand's Prime Minister Yingluck announced the dissolution of the nation's parliament and called a snap election to be held in February 2014. But this did not appease the thousands of angry protestors who remained on the streets of Bangkok.

During this time of social unrest, Prime Minister Yingluck were mostly absent from Bangkok to avoid protestors, spending more time in the Northern and Northeastern areas. It was in such a difficult time for the prime minister and the country of Thailand that Master Ryuho Okawa conducted a spiritual interview with Prime Minister Yingluck. In this spiritual interview, the guardian spirit of Prime Minister Yingluck shares her views on many controversial topics including democracy in Thailand, Thailand's relationships with China and Japan, traditional Buddhism, and Islam. She then asks Japan to help her country which has plunged into turmoil. It is Master Ryuho Okawa's hope that this interview will become a bridge to build a wonderful relationship between Thailand and Japan.

MOTHER TERESA'S CURRENT CALLING IN HEAVEN

THE SAINT OF THE GUTTERS DELIVERS HER EXPERIENCES OF GOD, HEAVEN, AND OUR MISSION

ISBN: 978-1-937673-55-0

$14.95 (Paperback)

This book is a spiritual interview with Mother Teresa's spirit who talks through Master Ryuho Okawa. In this spiritual interview, which was conducted sixteen years after Mother Teresa's death, Mother Teresa's spirit talks about her astonishing discoveries about God, Heaven, and the mission that people on earth should aim to fulfill through life. Mother Teresa reveals that the other world is a vast place with many levels of angels, that Heaven and Hell exist, and that the reality of the human being is the soul. In addition to a discussion about the contradictions within Christian teachings and the need for new teachings for today's people, she also talks about her discoveries about God and Jesus Christ, and says that it is the mission of the wealthy to help others who are in poverty, through prayer and a pure heart.

NELSON MANDELA'S LAST MESSAGE

A Conversation with Madiba
Six Hours After His Death

ISBN: 978-1-937673-53-6

$14.95 (Paperback)

On December 5, 2013, the entire world mourned the passing of Nelson Mandela. Even as the news was spreading, Mandela's spirit came to Master Ryuho Okawa to give us all an important message of hope and to prove that the afterlife exists. Archbishop of Canterbury Justin Wilby paid this tribute to the first black president of South Africa and the man who liberated his country from apartheid: "His courage was undefeated, indomitable, extraordinary." Perhaps it was Mandela's indomitable belief in the fundamental reality of the human soul that gave him such extraordinary courage in the face of adversity. For as he says in this spiritual interview, God created our souls as thinking energy without color, and that our colorless soul is the basis of our fundamental freedom and equality. In this spiritual interview, Master Ryuho Okawa gives us a glimpse into the mind of this great leader whose undefeated spirit is a message of hope to us all.

SOUTH KOREA'S CONSPIRACY

PRESIDENT PARK'S HIDDEN AGENDA TO UNITE WITH CHINA

ISBN: 978-1-937673-51-2

$14.95 (Paperback)

On June 27, 2013, South Korea's President Park Geun-hye and Chinese President Xi Jinping held summit talks in Beijing. At the meeting, President Park asked China's Xi Jinping to build a memorial of An Jung-geun, the man who in 1909 assassinated the first Prime Minister of Japan and the first Resident-General of Korea, Ito Hirobumi. In this spiritual interview, we begin by speaking with the spirit of An Jung-geun before moving on to a conversation with the guardian spirit of President Park, who forced herself into the interview out of fear that the interview will reveal the truth about him. Through these conversations, Master Ryuho Okawa tries to discover the facts about the assassination of Ito Hirobumi to determine whether An Jung-geun can justifiably be hailed as a hero. While South Koreans continue to accuse Japan of having wronged their nation, Master Okawa hopes that these interviews will provide a truthful understanding of the historical events between Japan and South Korea and help the international community understand the nature of true international justice.

MARGARET THATCHER'S
MIRACULOUS MESSAGE

AN INTERVIEW WITH THE IRON LADY
19 HOURS AFTER HER DEATH

ISBN: 978-1-937673-37-6

$14.95 (Paperback)

On April 9, 2013, just nineteen hours after Margaret Thatcher's death, Master Ryuho Okawa summoned her spirit to hold a miraculous spiritual interview with Europe's first female prime minister, famously known as the Iron Lady. In words marked by her signature clarity and determination, Margaret Thatcher provided valuable answers to essential and timely questions. Her answers will prove helpful not only to the United Kingdom, but also to the global economy and governments all over the world, including those of the United States and the European Union.

UNMASKING BAN KI-MOON'S BIASED STANCE

INVESTIGATING THE PARALYSIS OF THE UNITED NATIONS

ISBN: 978-1-937673-49-9

$14.95 (Paperback)

The world is currently facing many critical international issues that require resolution through strong leadership dedicated to the preservation of international peace and security. What are U.N. Secretary-General Ban Ki-moon's true thoughts on these pressing issues? What does he think about the disputes between Japan and South Korea over ownership of the Takeshima Islands, between Japan and China over ownership of the Senkaku Islands, and between Iran and Israel over nuclear weapons capability? Can we depend on him to successfully uphold the principle of impartiality in the United Nations's role of peacemaking? In this spiritual interview with the guardian spirit of Mr. Ban Ki-moon, Master Okawa reveals the U.N. Secretary-General's true character and true intentions regarding his important peacemaking responsibilities.

STEVE JOBS RETURNS
WITH HIS SECRETS

BE SIMPLE, BE CRAZY

ISBN: 978-1-937673-47-5

$19.95 (Paperback)

In this spiritual interview with Steve Jobs, conducted just three months after his death, Master Okawa offers us a chance to catch a glimpse into the mind of one of America's modern geniuses, whom President Barack Obama has described as one among the greatest American innovators. What was the aesthetic philosophy behind his passionate drive to create products that he described as "at the intersection of art and technology?" What were the secrets to his creativity and the successful sales of his products? As Master Okawa often says, and as this interview with the mind of one of the greatest modern innovators will show you, success is always in the way we think and in the substance of our goals and ideals.

THE SYRIAN CRISIS

WHAT IS GOD'S VERDICT ON U.S. MILITARY INTERVENTION?

ISBN: 978-1-937673-44-4

$14.95 (Paperback)

Is there justice in a U.S. military intervention into the ongoing Syrian crisis? What is God's perspective on the tragedy that is occurring in Syria? In *The Syrian Crisis: What Is God's Verdict on U.S. Military Intervention?* Master Ryuho Okawa conducts a spiritual interview with the guardian spirit of Bashar al-Assad. As this interview reveals, the Syrian dictator's true character is quite different from what we saw in the CBS interview. As the world braces for a possible world war, Master Ryuho Okawa provides us with a clear sense of where God's justice lies in this international crisis.

THE JUST CAUSE IN THE IRAQ WAR

DID SADDAM HUSSEIN POSSESS
WEAPONS OF MASS DESTRUCTION?

ISBN: 978-1-937673-41-3

$14.95 (Paperback)

The Just Cause in the Iraq War: Did Saddam Hussein Possess Weapons of Mass Destruction? tackles one of the most controversial and pertinent issues in international politics today. Is President Obama correct that the Iraq War was an unjust war, as he claimed during the 2012 presidential race? Did Saddam Hussein truly have no weapons of mass destruction, or are those weapons still hidden in Iraq, somewhere beyond the reach of U.S. intelligence? In this book, you will discover that Saddam Hussein was also behind the planning of the 9/11 terrorist attacks and both he and Osama bin Laden are now in Hell. The knowledge this book provides will help each of us make the right decisions as we work together to create a peaceful international society.

FORECASTING THE SECOND KOREAN WAR

HOW WILL THE WORLD HANDLE THE CRISIS?

ISBN: 978-1-937673-35-2

$14.95 (Paperback)

Forecasting the Second Korean War: How Will the World Handle the Crisis? forecasts a potential crisis that the United States, South Korea, and Japan may face. In part 1, Master Okawa draws on the help of Edgar Cayce to describe in detail the unfolding of a second Korean War that could begin in the summer of 2013. Part 2 of this book contains a spiritual interview with Kim Il Sung that reveals that he is spiritually guiding Kim Jong Un. Together, the two parts of this book reveal the shocking fact that the crisis on the Korean peninsula is only a small part of a larger and more global imperialistic scheme that is being masterminded by Xi Jinping, the president of China. You will discover who is truly behind the Islamist terrorist attacks against the United States.

EXPOSING NORTH KOREA'S MENACING LEADER

KIM JONG UN'S PLOT FOR A PSYCHOLOGICAL WAR

ISBN: 978-1-937673-39-0

$14.95 (Paperback)

Exposing North Korea's Menacing Leader: Kim Jong Un's Plot for a Psychological War reveals the role that North Korea is playing in China's imperialistic strategy and the two nations' close ties with Iran. Together, China and Kim Jong Un—North Korea's supreme leader— are carrying out a psychological war that takes full advantage of the weaknesses of Japanese Prime Minister Abe and United States President Obama. Indeed, this interview with Kim Jong Un's guardian spirit reveals that Kim Jong Un was most likely behind the Boston marathon bombings that occurred on April 15, 2013.

THE IRAN-ISRAEL CRISIS

LOOKING FOR A WAY TO PREVENT A NUCLEAR WAR

ISBN: 978-1-937673-26-0

$14.95 (Paperback)

Master Ryuho Okawa firmly believes that the power to create lasting global peace will come from embracing love and forgiveness beyond differences in religion. This set of spiritual interviews with the guardian spirits of Iran's President Mahmoud Ahmadinejad and Israel's Prime Minister Benjamin Netanyahu reveal their living counterparts' underlying ideas about each other's nations as arch enemies. You will discover hints to solving long-standing clashes between religions.

CHINA'S SECRET MILITARY BASES

A REMOTE-VIEWING INVESTIGATION
OF SUSPICIOUS SATELLITE IMAGES

ISBN: 978-1-937673-24-6

$14.95 (Paperback)

Master Okawa reveals China's versions of Area 51 from mysterious satellite photos that had aroused worldwide curiosity. Even American intelligence will be shocked to find out these truths about a hidden enormous missile-launching site full of nuclear warheads prepared to strike major cities around the world. This book is a must-read for anyone who wants to save the world from a full-out nuclear war.

HAVE FAITH IN GREAT AMERICA

LIBERTY AND WORLD JUSTICE FOR ALL

ISBN: 978-1-937673-20-8

$14.95 (Paperback)

Have Faith in Great America: Liberty and World Justice for All is Master Ryuho Okawa's earnest message to the United States of America. The world's future depends on America's fulfillment of its long-held sacred mission of protecting the faith, liberty, and justice of people and nations around the world, and on the development of strong bonds between the United States and Japan.

CHINA'S HIDDEN AGENDA

THE MASTERMIND BEHIND THE ANTI-AMERICAN
AND ANTI-JAPANESE PROTESTS

ISBN: 978-1937673-18-5

$14.95 (Paperback)

"Anti-American demonstrations have been raging in over twenty Arab countries. The man pulling the strings behind all this is Xi Jinping."

—Master Ryuho Okawa

"I wanted to stir up the anti-American movement in the Arab world to make sure that the United States won't be able to attack Syria or Iran...I'm the mastermind behind the Muhammad video."

—Xi Jinping's Guardian Spirit

PRESIDENT PUTIN AND
THE FUTURE OF RUSSIA

An Interview with the Guardian Spirit
of Vladimir Putin

ISBN: 978-1-937673-14-7

$14.95 (Paperback)

"I have no intention of fighting the United States. The Cold War is over... I have no intention of fighting the Americans... And I'm not friendly enough with China to think about joining them against the United States... I have given Russians religious freedom, which makes me very different from the Chinese."
—Putin's Guardian Spirit